Darkness into Light

by Mary Miller

PEARSON

Scott
Foresman

Editorial Offices: Glenview, Illinois • Parsippany, New Jersey • New York, New York
Sales Offices: Needham, Massachusetts • Duluth, Georgia • Glenview, Illinois
Coppell, Texas • Ontario, California • Mesa, Arizona

Every effort has been made to secure permission and provide appropriate credit for photographic material. The publisher deeply regrets any omission and pledges to correct errors called to its attention in subsequent editions.

Unless otherwise acknowledged, all photographs are the property of Scott Foresman, a division of Pearson Education.

Photo locators denoted as follows: Top (T), Center (C), Bottom (B), Left (L), Right (R), Background (Bkgd)

Opener: Brand X Pictures; 3 Getty Images; 4 Getty Images; 6 Digital Wisdom; 7 Brand X Pictures; 8 Digital Wisdom; 10 Brand X Pictures; 12 Getty Images; 113 Brand X Pictures; 15 Brand X Pictures; 16 Brand X Pictures; 17 Brand X Pictures; 18 Brand X Pictures; 19 Brand X Pictures

ISBN: 0-328-13449-X

11 12 13 14 15 16 V0FL 15 14 13 12 11

Day Turns into Night

On Earth, each full day is twenty-four hours long. In many places, daylight lasts longer in the summer than it does in the winter. But this pattern is not the same everywhere. In some places, the length of daylight or nighttime darkness can be extreme. During summer, daylight can last until midnight. During winter, nighttime can last for six months.

Countries with extreme day and night cycles are close to Earth's North and South Poles. To understand day and night on Earth, we need to look at Earth's place in the solar system.

Day

Night

Earth's Revolution

Our solar system has one sun and eight planets. The planets revolve, or travel, around the sun. Different planets take different lengths of time to orbit, or circle, the sun. For example, Mercury makes one trip around the sun in eighty-eight days. Mercury's trip is the shortest because Mercury is the closest planet to the sun. The movement of a planet all the way around the sun is called a revolution.

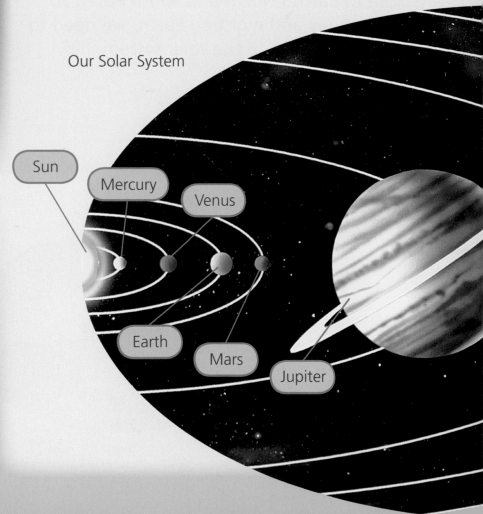

Our Solar System

Sun

Mercury

Venus

Earth

Mars

Jupiter

Earth is the third planet from the sun. This location makes it possible for Earth to have an environment in which humans, plants, and animals can live and grow. Earth takes 365 days, or one year, to make a revolution. During this time, people on Earth experience winter, spring, summer, and fall. The position of Earth as it makes a revolution causes seasons.

Uranus

Saturn

Neptune

Earth's Rotation

Earth is in a tilted position. As Earth orbits the sun, it is tilted and rotates, or spins, on its axis. The axis is an imaginary line running from the North Pole through the center of Earth to the South Pole. Earth spins around on this imaginary line.

Our planet spins very fast—about one thousand miles an hour. Because the speed never changes, we don't feel the movement. Earth takes twenty-four hours, or one day, to complete one rotation.

North Pole

Axis

South Pole

Light from the sun only falls on one-half of Earth at a time. The side of Earth facing the sun has daylight. The other side of Earth is in shadow, or darkness. As Earth spins, we move from day to night and back again.

In twenty-four hours, there is sunrise, daylight, sunset, and nighttime. As Earth begins to turn toward the sun, it is sunrise. When Earth begins to turn away from the sun, the sun seems to set.

Divided Up

The equator is an imaginary line that runs horizontally around the middle of Earth. It divides the planet into a Northern and a Southern Hemisphere. North of the equator is another imaginary line called the Tropic of Cancer. South of the equator is a third imaginary line called the Tropic of Capricorn. The area between them is called the Tropics.

The Tropics do not have much change in temperature. During Earth's orbit, the sun's rays constantly reach this central area of the globe, so this area is usually very warm.

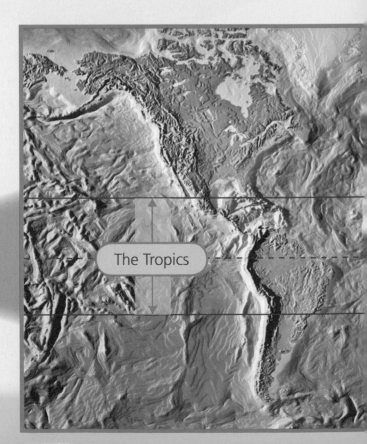

The Tropics

Areas north of the Tropic of Cancer or south of the Tropic of Capricorn have greater changes in climate. The weather is warmer in the hemisphere that is tilted toward the sun. In the hemisphere tilted away from the sun, the weather is cooler. The sun's energy can't reach the areas tilted away from it as directly as it can hit the areas tilted toward it.

The part of the Northern or Southern Hemisphere that is most tilted away from the sun has an extremely cold winter. And while the Tropics are usually warm in every season, the summers in this area are very hot.

Tropic of Cancer

The equator

Tropic of Capricorn

Solstices

Around June 22, summer solstice, the sun is directly over the Tropic of Cancer. On this day, the Northern Hemisphere has the most hours of daylight. The Northern Hemisphere is tilted toward the sun. Summer solstice is the start of summer in the Northern Hemisphere and the start of winter in the Southern Hemisphere. As Earth continues its orbit, the Northern Hemisphere begins to tilt away from the sun. There are fewer and fewer hours of daylight.

Around December 22, winter solstice, the sun is directly over the Tropic of Capricorn. On this day, the Northern Hemisphere has the fewest hours of daylight. The Northern Hemisphere is now tilted away from the sun.

Summer Solstice
June 22

Winter solstice is the start of winter in the Northern Hemisphere and summer in the Southern Hemisphere. Australia, in the Southern Hemisphere, has summertime in the month of December! After the winter solstice, there are more hours of daylight each day.

At the equator, daylight and nighttime are twelve hours each. As you move away from the equator toward the poles, the lengths of daylight and nighttime change. When it is summer in the Northern Hemisphere, daylight is longer and nighttime is shorter. In the winter, daylight is shorter and nighttime is longer. The closer you get to the poles, the more the amounts of daylight and darkness change.

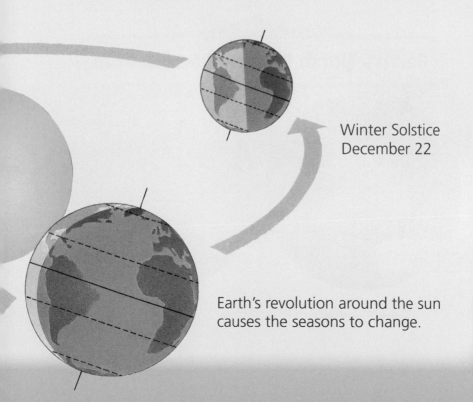

Winter Solstice
December 22

Earth's revolution around the sun causes the seasons to change.

The Poles

The Arctic is one of the coldest places on Earth. The Arctic is the northernmost part of the world—the land and oceans around the North Pole. It includes parts of Alaska, Canada, Greenland, Norway, Russia, and the Arctic Ocean.

The South Pole is in Antarctica. The continent of Antarctica makes up most of the Antarctic. Seasons and times of day and night at the South Pole are opposite to those of the North Pole. Because of Earth's tilt in its orbit, daylight lasts for six months at the pole that is tilted toward the sun. This period of daylight is followed by a six-month nighttime.

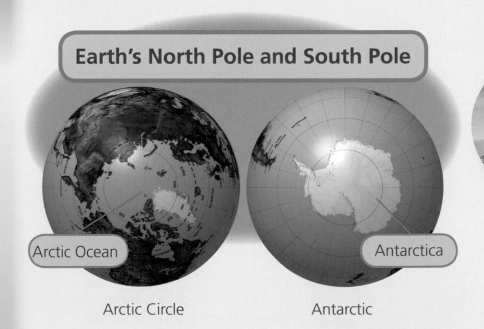

Earth's North Pole and South Pole

Arctic Ocean

Antarctica

Arctic Circle

Antarctic

The Arctic

There are extreme changes in seasons and day and night in the Arctic. Some Arctic places have days in the summer when the sun never sets. In the winter, some places in the Arctic have twenty-four hours of darkness for weeks at a time. Because of the dark and cold, ice and snow cover most of the land. Places in the Antarctic have conditions similar to the Arctic, but the conditions happen at opposite times of the year.

The Arctic has extremely cold temperatures.

Animal Life in the Arctic

Animals are adapted to survive in the Arctic environment. Caribou, polar bears, wolverines, musk oxen, and arctic foxes roam the barren lands. Killer whales prowl the icy waters.

Polar bears spend their days either on land, on packed ice, or in the frigid water. Their white fur lets them sneak up on prey, such as seals, lying on the ice. The bears hunt all summer long. During the harshest days of winter, the bears hibernate in dens.

Walruses are also able to stay warm in the Arctic cold. They have layers of blubber under their hides. The fat keeps them warm from the cold winds. Walruses are noisy animals. They make a **chorus** of loud, bellowing sounds as they crowd together on the ice. Although they are timid, walruses are not **cowards.** If one member of the herd is attacked, other walruses will protect it.

Walruses and polar bears live in the Arctic.

Life in Iceland

The island of Iceland lies just below the Arctic Circle. The country is far enough away from the North Pole to be spared six full months of nighttime in the winter. But still, winters in Iceland are long and dark. In December and January, there are no more than three or four hours of sunlight each day. Villages in the country's deep valleys do not see the sun at all during the long winter months.

Map of Iceland

Icelanders have adapted to their surroundings. The waters around Iceland are filled with a variety of fish. The fishing industry is a source of employment for many. Fish and fish products make up the country's most important export. Icelanders have found different ways to use natural energy sources. They use hydropower, or water power. They also use geothermal power, power produced by heat from inside Earth.

Landscapes of Iceland

Northern Lights

Winter holds a special treat for Icelanders. These dark months are the best time to see a natural wonder known as the Northern Lights. This light show is called the *aurora borealis.* The **brilliant, shimmering** green light spreads across the sky in streaks, arcs, and clouds. It shows viewers the sun's activity in the atmosphere.

A similar light show can be seen in the Southern Hemisphere. There it is called the *aurora australis,* or Southern Lights. In the Antarctic, sheets of green and pink light dance across the night sky.

Aurora borealis

Return of the Sun

When summer arrives in Iceland, the sun shines through most of the night. Most of Iceland sees the sun settle just below the horizon at midnight. A long dusk is the only sign that a day has ended.

After the long winter, many Icelanders enjoy outdoor activities during June and July. It is not unusual to see young children playing outside under a sun that **gleamed** at midnight! What are the days and nights like where you live?

A summer night in Iceland

Glossary

brilliant *adj.* shining brightly; sparkling.

chorus *n.* anything spoken or sung all at the same time.

cowards *n.* people or animals that lack courage or are easily made afraid.

gleamed *v.* flashed or beamed with light.

shimmering *adj.* gleaming faintly.